VA DISABILITY CLAIM APPROVED!

A Step by Step Guide on How to Win Your VA Benefits!

MY VA BENEFITS SERIES – BOOK 1

GraceHaven Publishing

Copyright 2018

ISBN: 9781983102677

Table of Contents

□

Introduction

First, let me start by thanking you for your Military Service.
Regardless when or where you served, by virtue of the fact that you
were willing to sacrifice all that you hold dear to ensure the freedom
of your fellow countrymen reveals your true dedication to our great
country. For that, I salute you! Moreover, because of your
honorable service to protect our way of life, we as a Country
incurred a debt to take care of you. However, for many of our
military brothers and sisters, I believe the VA has not upheld its side
of the bargain and it saddens me that a book of this nature is even
necessary. But be heartened, for despite a previous VA denial, if
you are able to meet the requirements as spelled out in this book, you
WILL win the benefits and entitlements that you deserve!

I served nearly 27 years in the U.S. Air Force and then another 10 years in my "second career" as a Veterans Service Officer (VSO.) Now for my third and hopefully final "career," I plan on taking it easy and writing books to continue my advocacy for Veterans, for the knowledge I gained during those 10 years as a VSO, I believe, is far too important NOT to continuing sharing with other disabled Veterans.

As a VSO, I spent four years advocating for Veterans benefits at the St Petersburg VA Regional Office, another four and a half years working with patients at the James H. Haley VA Medical Center in Tampa, and then the last year and a half providing community-based advocacy for our Veterans in and around Sumter County Florida.

As a result of this experience, I not only became familiar with VA law and the VA disability claims and appeals processes, I learned the procedural matrixes the decision makers (Raters, Decision Review Officers, and Judges) utilize to adjudicated disability claims. As a result of that experience, I discovered that by approaching the Veterans benefits process from the perspective of what could be granted, instead of focusing on what would be denied, I could help Veterans become VICTORS instead of victims.

As I assessed the numerous self-help books out there related to VA disability claims and appeals, I found several that do a pretty good job addressing the claims and appeals process and how to submit a claim, but I could not find very much specific information on how to address and develop the NEXUS or link necessary for a VA disability claim. This will be the first book of what I am calling the **"MY VA BENEFITS SERIES."**

Subsequent books in this series will address such topics as how to submit a fully developed claim, how to prepare for your Compensation and Pension Examination, additional benefits you didn't know you were entitled to, VA benefits for surviving spouses and children, and more. So whether you are seeking a reconsideration of a recent disability claim or your disability claim is currently in the appeals process, this information is vital to ensuring you have the knowledge necessary to win the veterans benefits you deserve!

I would be very interested in hearing of your success. If there is something that I've written that is not clear, I would like to know that too. Please reach out to me via email and I will respond as soon as possible. rickblairbooks@gmail.com.

* * *

Now that I am retired, I do consult with Veterans who want personalized guidance with their Nexus letter(s.) If you are having difficulty crafting your NEXUS letter, reach out to me at rickblairbooks@gmail.com and we can discuss your specific need.

* * *

PERSONAL REQUEST

I humbly ask that if you feel that this book has been beneficial to you in learning how to write a winning NEXUS letter, that you write a **POSITIVE REVIEW** so that others might be convinced that they too, can obtain the VA benefits they deserve.

☐

* * *

Chapter 1

Purpose of the NEXUS Letter

Simply put, the primary purpose of your NEXUS letter is to explain the link between your current disability and your military service. However, it also has another very important role, and that is to establish a "benefit of doubt" between your claim and the VA's decision. My supervisor shared baseball as an analogy to explain the precept of the NEXUS letter. When a runner is legging out a ground ball to first base, if the ball and the runner arrives at the same time, the Umpire rules the runner safe, because the "tie goes to the runner." However, if there isn't a tie, the Umpire doesn't call the runner safe, simply because "he was close enough."

As in this analogy, your claim has to have an approximate balance of positive and negative evidence before the VA's benefit of the doubt rule can apply. This is not a matter of questioning your integrity or your supporting evidence on whether the facts are "close enough," it all comes down to whether you can establish an actual "tie" with the VA.

According to the statute 38 USC § 5107(b), "The Secretary [VA] shall consider all information and lay and medical evidence of record in a case before the Secretary [VA] with respect to benefits under laws administered by the Secretary [VA]. When there is an approximate balance of positive and negative evidence regarding any issue material to the determination of a matter, the Secretary [VA] shall give the benefit of the doubt to the claimant."

The benefit of the doubt – also known as the Reasonable Doubt – is further clarified by 38 CFR §3.102, which states that "the Department of Veterans Affairs [is] to administer the law under a broad interpretation, consistent, however, with the facts shown in every case. When, after careful consideration of all procurable and assembled data, a reasonable doubt arises regarding service origin, the degree of disability, or any other point, such doubt will be resolved in favor of the claimant. By reasonable doubt is meant one which exists because of an approximate balance of positive and negative evidence which does not satisfactorily prove or disprove the claim. It is a substantial doubt and one within the range of probability as distinguished from pure speculation or remote possibility. It is not a means of reconciling actual conflict or a contradiction in the evidence. Mere suspicion or doubt as to the truth of any statements submitted, as distinguished from impeachment or contradiction by evidence or known facts, is not justifiable basis for denying the application of the reasonable doubt doctrine if the entire complete record otherwise warrants invoking this doctrine. The reasonable doubt doctrine is also applicable even in the absence of official records, particularly if the basic incident allegedly arose under combat, or similarly strenuous conditions, and is consistent with the probable results of such known hardships." [Emphasis mine.]

38 CFR §4.3 adds further insight to the benefit of the doubt doctrine when it affirms that When after careful consideration of all procurable and assembled data, a reasonable doubt arises regarding the degree of disability such doubt will be resolved in favor of the claimant. [Emphasis mine.]

Wow! Did you get all that? Basically, this means that if you can provide a NEXUS letter that approximates a balance of positive evidence to the VA's negative opinion, the VA has to grant your claim! So what does that look like? How DO you go about providing the positive evidence needed to balance the scale of evidence?

The majority of the time, the reason for the VA's denial comes down to a negative medical opinion provided by the VA doctor during your Compensation and Pension (C&P) examination.

Because the VA has already provided the NEGATIVE evidence by denying your claim, it is now up to you to provide the POSITIVE evidence to reach that level of APPROXIMATE BALANCE so that "a reasonable doubt arises regarding service origin, the degree of disability, or any other point, such doubt will be resolved in favor of the claimant."

The good news is that the VA has already tipped their hand as to why they believe your current disability is not linked to your military service or service connected disability. The specific reason for their denial should be listed in your rating decision, or if it is poorly written and not articulated there, it will definitely be in the compensation and pension examination report describing the VA doctor's findings from your examination.

Remember, the compensation and pension examination report is a part of your VA medical records and you have a right to request it from the medical facility that produced it.

Occasionally, the VA medical facility will put a hold on a Psychological compensation and pension examination until the rating decision is finalized, but once the decision has been adjudicated and released, they have to provide you with that examination record.

But I'm getting ahead of myself, let's start from the beginning so that it is clear why and how your doctor's NEXUS letter will be the key to winning your claim.

How the VA Rates a Claim

There are eight distinct steps within VA disability claims process. These steps or phases may vary in length depending on the complexity of the claim, the amount of evidence that must be gathered to support the claim, and the type of evidence needed. The eight steps of claim processing are as follows:

Step 1. Claim Received

Regardless whether you apply for your claim online or through a traditional submission method (mail, VSO, etc.), once the VA receives your claim they "date stamp" the claim to establish an effective date and proof of receipt. It is logged into the appropriate claim category or "queue" and waits for initial review. It is always a good idea to follow up on your claim within a month or so of submission to ensure the claim actually made it to the VA and is acknowledged as "received."

Step 2. Under Review

When your claim reaches the top of its queue, it is assigned to a Veterans Service Representative (VSR) to begin developing the claim and to determine if additional evidence is needed. The VSR will make a tracking list of information needed for the Rater to make a ruling on your claim. If you have submitted a fully developed claim, it is sent directly to the Preparation for Decision phase. The topic of "How to prepare a fully developed claim" is outside the scope of this book, but I will be writing a subsequent book on the subject. If you don't want to wait for the book to come out, you can research the VA website, or find a competent VSO in your area to assist you if you wish to go that route.

Step 3. Gathering of Evidence

The VSR will identify and request evidence from the required sources that archive your information. Examples of request for evidence may include private medical doctors, various governmental agencies, or even from you. When a request for information is sent out, the VA typically sets a future suspense date of 30 - 60 days. If the information is not received within that timeframe, usually a second request will be sent. You will also be notified that the VA is having difficulty obtaining this information and offered the opportunity to gather and submit the evidence yourself.

It is usually during this step that the Veteran's Claim Assistance Act Letter (more commonly known as the Duty to Assist Letter) is mailed to you. This letter basically advises you of the VA's duty to help you with your claim. This topic is discussed in further detail in the Bonus Chapter at the end of this book.

Step 4. Review of Evidence

Once the VA receives all evidence they've identified as relevant to your claim (or determined that the information is not available and further efforts to pursue the information would be futile), the VSR will review the evidence to determine if it is complete. If, upon review, it is determined that more evidence is required, the claim will be redirected back to Step 2, the Gathering of Evidence phase.

Step 5. Preparation for Decision

Once the VSR has determined that all evidence has been received, the claim will be forwarded to a Rater for review. If the rater determines no more information is needed to make a decision, the claim will be marked "ready to rate." However, if the Rater determines that more evidence is required, for example clarification of a medical opinion is needed, the claim will again be redirected back to Step 2, the Gathering of Evidence phase.

Step 6. Pending Decision Approval

Once the Rater has determined that your claim is complete and "ready to rate," he will make a decision on your claim. That recommended decision is reviewed, and assuming no mistakes were found, a final award is made. Again, if during this review process it is determined that more evidence or information is required, the claim will be redirected back to Step 2, the Gathering of Evidence phase.

Step 7. Preparation for Notification

At this point, a notification letter is generated and additional information provided to advise you of your rights if you do not agree with the VA's determination regarding your award. .

Step 8. Complete

Once the VA sends out their rating decision by U.S. mail, the claim is considered complete and your file is closed out.

How Long Does This Process Take?

The length of time it takes to complete a claim depends on several factors, such as the type of claim filed, the number of disabilities you claim, the complexity of your disability(ies), and the availability of evidence needed to decide your claim. In recent years, the VA was criticized for how long it was taking to finalize claims and significant effort and resources were expended to reduce the backlog of claims and the time it takes to make a decision. By investing in technological advances and establishing better workflow efficiencies, the VA has made significant headway in their goals to reduce the number of days it takes to process claims. In my opinion, the next big hurdle the VA needs to address will be shortening the length of time it's taking to address appeals, which currently takes several years to finalize. The VA has announced a plan that they hope will be finalized and implemented by the spring of 2019, so hopefully the new process will significantly improve the appeals process as well.

How the VA Determines Probability

So now that we have a working idea of how the claim process works, let's look at how the VA decides your claim. When it comes to making a final decision on your claim, after reviewing the merits of all the compiled, relevant information, the VA Rater uses probability to determine whether your claim is related to your military service. The word they use to determine that probability is "likely" and any other synonym to "likely" is not accepted; possibly, probably, maybe, might, perhaps, could be, conceivably, appears to be, plausible, feasible – the list could go on and on. Although these words are often used in doctors' opinions and imply a level of confidence that would clearly indicate to the average person that the doctor is providing a positive opinion, they are not accepted by the VA.

As such, when providing an opinion, your doctor should mirror the language that the VA uses so that "apples can be compared to apples." The following is how the VA determines probability:

- "is due to / is caused by" = (100% percent probable)

- "more likely than not" = (greater than 50% percent probable)

- "at least as likely as not" = (equal to or greater than 50% percent probable)

- "less likely as not" = (less than 50% percent probable)

- "is not due to / is not caused by"= (0% percent probable)

As you can see, there are five levels of probability as far as the VA is concerned. However, only two of them are ever REALLY necessary when determining the approximate balance of positive and negative evidence; "less likely as not" (negative) and "at least as likely as not" (positive.) It doesn't matter if the VA states that there is a 0% percent chance that your disability was caused by your military service, if your doctor provides a NEXUS letter that shows a 50% percent probability and all "other factors" (relevant evidence) are approximately equal, the benefit of the doubt doctrine should be invoked and you should win your claim! We'll address specifics in Chapter 4 as to how and why these "other factors" (relevant evidence) need to be addressed so that they represent an approximate balance to the VA. But you need to remember, while it may be satisfying to your ego that your doctor states "more likely than not" in his letter, that does not make any more difference to the Benefit of Doubt doctrine than if he merely states "at least as likely as not," because a 50% percent probability is considered positive to the VA! We'll get into this more when we discuss the doctor's role in Chapter 3.

Special Purpose for a NEXUS Letter

As many of you know, when a claim is submitted and denied, you have one year to do something about that denial; either by submitting a reconsideration or requesting an appeal. If you do nothing within that one year period, the claim becomes "final." As such, if you wish to "reopen" your claim, you must provide "new and material evidence."

According to 38 CFR 3.156, "a claimant may reopen a finally adjudicated claim by submitting new and material evidence. New evidence means existing evidence not previously submitted to agency decision makers. Material evidence means existing evidence that, by itself or when considered with previous evidence of record, relates to an unestablished fact necessary to substantiate the claim. **New and material evidence can be neither cumulative nor redundant of the evidence of record at the time of the last prior final denial of the claim sought to be reopened, and must raise a reasonable possibility of substantiating the claim.**" [Emphasis mine]

In layman's terms, the NEW part of this requirement is that evidence that the VA has not seen before, which is generally very easy to provide. However, the MATERIAL part of the evidence is usually the sticking point. For example, if your claim was previously denied because you could not find missing records and they suddenly became available, then the MATERIAL piece would be easy. But typically, the problem is that you simply did not know that you only had a year to respond or became disgusted with the VA's decision and chucked it in the trash and went on with your life; once that year passed the date of the Rater's decision, it became "final." As such, having your doctor provide a NEXUS letter now meets both criteria to reopen your claim; it is new, the VA has not seen it before AND it's material because it "relates to an unestablished fact necessary to substantiate the claim." Moreover, once the claim is reopened, the VA must then consider your Doctor's opinion as it applies to the Benefit of Doubt doctrine, which is what you wanted all along.

Now that we've examined the goal of the NEXUS letter, let's briefly explore the VA's most common reasons for denying a claim, so we can see how the NEXUS letter fits into how you will submit your claim or respond to an appeal.

Chapter 2

Common Reasons for Denial

Assuming that you don't have a regulatory or statutory bar that disqualifies you from receiving VA benefits (i.e., negative circumstances surrounding your military discharge), the VA requires the following criteria be met to receive disability compensation:

- You must have a current, chronic disability; AND

- the disability must have been caused by, the result of, or aggravated by your military service or a secondary condition that was caused by an existing service connected disability; AND

- there must be a NEXUS or link between the first two criteria.

Sounds simple, right? Sadly, it's not always that easy when dealing with the VA. As we discussed in the previous chapter, when the VA considers your disability claim, they are determining the probability of whether your claim was caused by, the result of, or aggravated by your military service or a service connected disability. In the vast majority of claims, the reason for denial comes down to a negative VA doctor's opinion. Let's explore each of the specific criteria noted above and reasons the VA might deny, so that we can better under the purpose of the NEXUS letter.

No current (or undiagnosed), chronic condition

The first requirement for consideration of a VA disability claim is to have a current, chronic condition. While it would seem that this requirement is self-explanatory, with the VA, nothing is always as it seems. By "current," the VA requires that your disability or condition has existed for at least six months at the time of the disability claim.

While this definition seems intuitive, my experience has been that the VA has interpreted this requirement rather narrowly at times. For example, a Veteran submitted a disability claim for allergic rhinitis about 3 years after he separated from active duty. His service treatment records contained several entries clearly documenting a diagnosis of, and treatment for his "allergies" throughout the four years that he was in the Air Force. However, when he went to the VA compensation and pension examination, his symptoms were not obviously evident, because he self-treated with over-the-counter medications. As such, the VA doctor stated that the Veteran did not have a current condition. Moreover, he opined that the Veteran's allergies were "seasonal" and thereby not chronic in nature.

In another example, a Vietnam combat Veteran submitted a claim for diabetes mellitus type II, a presumptive condition caused by exposure to the herbicide Agent Orange. The VA conceded that he served in Vietnam, was likely exposed to the defoliant, and that diabetes was a presumptive condition, but denied his claim because he did not have a current diagnosis. The Veteran submitted his VA medical records that listed diabetes as a problem and his medications list showing that he was prescribed and taking Metformin, which is a drug used to treat diabetes. The VA examiner stated that in a review of his recent lab work, his A1C level was only at 6.3 and a reading of 6.5 was required for the VA to acknowledge a diagnosis of diabetes. Despite our argument that his Metformin was keeping his diabetes in check, the VA denied his claim because there was no laboratory finding that met their criteria for a diagnosis.

I could go on with other examples of where the VA denied claims based upon a negative finding of a current (undiagnosed) or chronic condition, but the point here is that sometimes, simply proving that you have a current disability can be a challenge.

Lacking proof of service event

This typically manifests itself in one of two ways; first, there is no medical evidence in your service treatment or military personnel records that record an event. This can often be a difficult problem to overcome, because many times it's not a matter of treatment, but a lack of documentation. This frequently happens when you are outside your permanent duty station; records are simply not produced or if they are, they do to get married up with your medical/personnel file at a later date. This is especially prevalent during field training exercises and in combat. As you know, a field medic's sole responsibility is to treat the wounded and get them back out to the front. Rarely is anything documented unless it requires treatment beyond the capabilities of the field medics, at which point you are transferred to the rear for more comprehensive care.

Interestingly, the VA denied one of my Veteran's claims because there was nothing recorded in his service treatment records concerning an injury he incurred during a field training exercise. Fortunately, he was able to find a copy of his PT profile limiting his duty immediately after that field exercise. With that documentation, he was able to demonstrate that he'd sustained the injury while in service.

The second way meeting this criteria can be a problem is when the VA feels the injury or condition noted in your service treatment records does not constitute a continuing disability. For example, you hurt your knee and your service treatment records indicates that you were seen in the clinic, diagnosed with a sprain, prescribed Ibuprofen, and put on light duty for two weeks.

However, if there are no further entries in your service treatment records specific to that knee injury OR it is not mentioned in your separation physical from the military, the VA's examiner will often assert that your knee injury was "resolved" and it was not the cause of your current knee problem. Moreover, even if there is adequate documentation and even perhaps a mention of the condition in your separation physical, if it has been an extended length of time since your separation from active duty and you cannot show continuing treatment of the disability, the VA will often argue that the condition was resolve. In a case like this, the VA is not refuting that you had an "incident" in service or that you have a current knee condition, they are simply stating that there is no substantial evidence that would indicate what happened in the service caused what you're dealing with now.

I remember a Veteran who injured his back while on active duty, was treated at the clinic a number of times, and he had even been issued several PT profiles limiting his duty. Additionally, the injury was even noted on the front (check block section) of his separation physical. Unfortunately, the Veteran could not find employment when he left the military and was unable to afford health insurance. A number of years later, he applied for and was granted Social Security Disability due primarily to his back condition.

He then applied for VA disability and was afforded a compensation and pension examination due to the numerous entries in his service treatment records. While the VA examiner acknowledged his service treatment records and noted current back pain during the examination, he specifically noted the lack of medical records from the time of his separation to present. He diagnosed the Veteran with "degenerative disc disease of the lower spine consistent with a male of his age" [emphasis mine.] As such, because the Veteran could not establish a chronicity of treatment for his back from the time he separated from active duty to the time he submitted his VA claim, the VA denied his back disability under the premise that his back must have been "resolved" since he did not seek continued treatment after his exit from the military AND the VA examiner's opinion that his condition was consistent with a male of his age.

It should be noted that a VA determination of a disability helps a Veteran with his Social Security claim, but in the majority of VA claims, a documented Social Security disability does not reciprocate with the VA. Simply put, with Social Security, you only needs to establish that your disabity(ies) preclude you from working, while the VA requires that you prove that the disability was caused by your military service. When the VA "service connects" you with a disability, Social Security will usually accept their findings and typically apply that disability toward their matrix. When you submit a VA claim, they will simply review your Social Security records as they would any other non-military treatment records.

No NEXUS or link

The last requirement needed for filing a VA claim is by far the most common reason a VA disability claim is denied. As noted above, you must established a NEXUS or link tying your claimed disability to your prior military service or existing service connected disability. Obviously, if the VA examiner agrees with your claim, then he in essence establishes the NEXUS for you. However in my experience, if the NEXUS is not abundantly clear within the medical evidence provided to the VA examiner, he will typically state that there is less likely than not (less than a 50/50 percent probability) that a NEXUS for your claim has been established.

For example, I hypothetically broke my shoulder while in the military, the doctor immobilized it for eight weeks, after which I was provided six weeks of physical therapy and then returned to full duty. After completing the remainder of my military obligation, I separated from active duty; this injury was noted on my separation physical. Ten years later, I begin having neuropathy issues down my arm and believe that scar tissue from my broken shoulder is the cause of the problem. If I submit a claim and have a current diagnosis for neuropathy, but cannot show a link between the broken shoulder in service and my current condition, the VA will deny the claim due to no NEXUS.

Even though the shoulder problem was noted on my separation physical, the VA would consider the condition to have been resolved, because of the length of time between the event in service and the time my neuropathy problem arose. Although there may be an apparent medical connection that seems reasonable to the average person, by law, the VA Rater cannot make that leap in logic. So if the VA examiner opines that he would have to resort to mere speculation to determine whether the neuropathy was caused by the previous shoulder break while in service, it has the same effect as a negative opinion and the Rater will deny the claim. NOTE: it is MY observation that this is a common practice with many VA examiners to avoid having to justify a negative opinion. I could continue with other examples, however, when we analyze the anatomy of a NEXUS letter in Chapter 4, I believe this concept will become abundantly clear.

But before we get into that, let's explore how and what to look for in a doctor who might be willing to write your NEXUS letter.

Chapter 3

Find a doctor to write your NEXUS Letter

Your VA doctor

If you receive VA health care, you can ask your doctor if he or she would be willing to assist you with the letter. However, you need to be prepared for the doctor to decline your request because the Veterans Health Administration discourages their doctors from providing claim support (see footnote below) . Over the years, I have been reprimanded by numerous VA doctors for encouraging my Veterans to ask them to sign a NEXUS letter. When I explained to the doctor why the Veteran is seeking a NEXUS and that he does not have access to private medical care, those doctors typically remained unmoved. I've even had one VA doctor tell me that his job was to provide medical treatment only and not to provide any other administrative support. As unfair as that may seem, it is a reality.

However, I have had some VA doctors who agreed to sign a NEXUS letter, especially if I wrote it for them to sign. So I always go back to encouraging the Veteran to ask his doctor – if you don't ask, the doctor can't say no!

Private Doctor

If your VA doctor will not sign a NEXUS letter, then you must find a private doctor who is willing to work with you AT YOUR OWN EXPENSE. Remember, although the VA has a duty to assist you with your claim (we cover this topic in the Bonus Chapter), it is still your claim to prove, thus it is YOUR responsibility to find a doctor willing to sign your NEXUS letter. If you have private medical insurance, you may be able to locate a doctor through their network.

I remember when I first submitted my claim, I wanted to be proactive with a NEXUS letter and submit that along with other medical evidence at the onset of my initial claim. I had private insurance (HMO) and needed to go through my primary care doctor for a consult to have my hearing examined. While I knew that the VA would be required to provide me a hearing exam (they conceded that I'd been subjected to acoustic trauma as a result of my job in the military), I wanted MY doctor to also provide a NEXUS letter. However, I also knew that I only had one shot with the doctor I chose, because if I picked a doctor who gave me an exam, but was not willing to sign a NEXUS, then my insurance company would not allow me to request another exam; I would have to pay for any subsequent exams out of pocket. So not wanting to leave it to chance, I decided to be proactive.

When my primary doctor agreed to an audiology consult, I got a list of doctors from the HMO website who were a part of my network plan and I started calling them. Of course I didn't get past the guard dog at the front desk, however, I explained that I wanted a private medical examination and opinion to support a VA claim that I was going to submit. I then asked if the doctor had been in the military or was supportive of the military. The first three offices I called said something like, "well, he was never in the military, but I'm sure he supports our troops!" Not satisfied that my odds had improved to much better than 50/50, I kept calling down the list. The fourth doctor is where I hit pay dirt! As soon as I explained what I needed, the receptionist said, "Oh I'm sure she will, her son is currently deployed to Iraq!" When I met with the doctor, we had an instant bond as a result of her son's military service and she signed the NEXUS letter without hesitation. The point here is not that I'm all that smart, but that you might have to be creative when you are looking for the right doctor!

Another option is to network with servicing organizations (such as DAV, American Legion, VFW, etc.) and other Veterans in your area to see if they know of a doctor who would work with you. Perhaps a Google search or local phone director could provide leads. Again, it is important to remember that if the doctor you use does not follow the acceptable VA standards needed in a NEXUS letter, then your attempt to establish an approximate balance of positive and negative evidence to invoke the Benefit of Doubt Rule will likely fail.

Concerns a Doctor Might Have in Writing a NEXUS Letter

A doctor will likely have questions and concerns when asked to write a NEXUS letter for you, especially if he is not familiar with the VA process or standards. Private physicians typically operate under the presumption of "medical certainty," which is a much higher standard than that required by the VA to determine the causality of a disability. As a result, private physicians are often hesitant in providing medical statements or if they do, may qualify their conclusions with vague terms such as "may," "could," "suggests," or "possibly." Again, as discussed previously, any word other than "likely" is not acceptable to the VA when determining probability.

If the NEXUS letter does not meet the VA standard, the claim will be denied, even if the physician's language indicates that he may actually believe the condition is likely service connected. Moreover, doctors are often concerned that they may be called before a VA or military medical board to defend their opinion. This will NOT happen, because the VA is only looking for an approximate balance of positive and negative evidence that "is inherently believable or has been received from a competent source." Because the doctor went to medical school and received his MD, he has earned the authority to provide a medical opinion that is within the realm of a 50/50 percent probability.

As such, his opinion will NOT need to be defended. As long as the doctor's opinion has "approximate probative value," as compared to the VA Compensation and Pension examiner's opinion, it will be accepted as credible medical evidence in support of the Veteran's quest of establishing the benefit of doubt. Remember, according to the CFR: "Approximate probative value" between a positive and negative opinion must be relevant to the issue in question AND have sufficient weight, either by itself or in combination with other evidence, to persuade the VA Rater about a fact.

Finally, because many doctors are unfamiliar with the VA process and standards, they are often concerned that providing a NEXUS letter, especially if the Veteran is not well known to the doctor, may jeopardize their Hippocratic Oath or medical license in some way. Again, this will NOT happen because the doctor is merely assessing whether there is a 50/50 percent probability that the Veteran's disability could have been caused by his military service or a service connected disability based solely upon the material evidence.

Overcoming a doctor's concerns

For many doctors, if there is an initial hesitation to write your NEXUS letter, even after addressing the major concerns mentioned above, he still may have unspoken concerns, such as time is money, he doesn't know what to write and he doesn't want to hurt your chances of winning your claim due to a poorly written letter.

I've found that my best success in overcoming a doctor's concerns was to offer to write the NEXUS letter so that he could decide for himself whether he would be comfortable signing his name to such a document. It's been my experience that when the doctor sees the letter and understands that what he will be signing is not only confined to a 50/50 percent probability, but supported by medical research from the National Institute of Health, he typically signs the letter as written. However, as you will see when we move into Chapter 4, if the doctor changes any of the substantive parts of the letter, then it could render your NEXUS useless; that is the risk you take when requesting his help.

What to Look for in a Doctor

I've often had Veterans ask me what kind of doctor they need to find. I tell them, "by and large, a doctor is a doctor is a doctor." While a specialist would always be preferred if reasonably available, most primary care, general practitioners, internal medicine and even physician assistants and nurse practitioners will usually suffice (the VA often utilizes physical assistants to conduct their Compensation and Pension examinations.) The major exception to this general statement is for mental disabilities; typically, the VA will only accept a psychiatrist's or psychologist's opinion and not a licensed mental health social worker (unless you are already service connected for a mental disability and merely looking for an increased evaluation.) Additionally, an audiologist is needed for hearing disabilities, and I've personally had cases where the Rater required an optometrist for ocular problems and an oncologist's opinion to determine service connection for certain cancers. However, I could probably count the times one of my Veterans needed to find a specialist on both hands.

Of course there are always those unusual circumstances where the VA denies a claim because the Rater states the VA doctor had more probative value to his opinion than the Veteran's doctor. I remember a time where the Veteran's claim for a back disability was denied because the VA doctor was an MD, while the Veteran's doctor was ONLY a chiropractor (a PhD with 20+ years of treating just the spine!) I probably could've won the claim on appeal, but fortunately, in addition to receiving VA care, the Veteran also had access to private insurance through his wife's company, so he merely had his wife's primary care doctor (who was sympathetic to his cause) sign the same NEXUS letter that his chiropractor had signed. We submitted the claim for reconsideration, arguing that now there should be no question regarding the probative value of the Veteran's doctor, because both doctors providing opinions were MD's. It worked out in this situation, but as you can see, a Veteran who is not as blessed to have access to a private doctor would've had to appeal the denial simply because the Rater had a bias.

Now, for the moment you've been waiting for! Let's explore the anatomy of a NEXUS letter.

Chapter 4

Anatomy of a NEXUS Letter

As we discussed in Chapter 1, the primary purpose of the NEXUS letter is explain the link between your current disability and your military service. However, the NEXUS letter is also used to demonstrate how your doctor is qualified to provide an approximate balance of positive evidence AND invoke the "benefit of doubt" (reasonable doubt) between your claim and the VA's negative decision.

As such, the NEXUS letter must establish the fact that YOUR doctor has reviewed the same or approximately the same evidence to formulate his positive opinion as the VA examiner did to conclude his negative opinion. If this is not demonstrated, the Rater will state in your denial letter something to the effect that "the VA examiner's opinion is deemed more credible because he was able to review your entire Claim file, while [your doctor] only had access to some of your medical records and your reported history from which to formulate his opinion."

While at the St Petersburg Regional Office, I routinely defended Veterans' claims by demonstrating to the appellate Judges that despite not having access to the Veteran's claim file, the Veteran's private doctor DID have access to enough RELEVENT evidence to formulate an opinion that had the approximate probative value as that of the VA examiner. However many times, all this frustration and delay could be avoided if the relevant evidence had simply been established up front in a NEXUS letter.

So let's first look at the NEXUS as a whole, then we'll break down and discuss the individual components. It should go without saying, but I just want to clarify; A NEXUS letter is a medical record, so it should be provided by a medical professional who is qualified to make the opinion.

A solid NEXUS letter should be dated, (1) identify the patient and (2) confirm the condition for which the doctor is providing (3) assessment/treatment, establish what information has been reviewed, (4) provide an opinion as to the cause of that malady, list applicable (5) medical research to support the doctor's opinion, acknowledge and (6) (7) address any conflicting opinions or etiology(ies), provide any other (8) relevant information, close by reiterating the opinion, and provide a (9) (10) signature, title and Medical Examiner number. (11)

I should probably note here that some of my VSO peers have argued that the Doctor's specific medical qualifications should be provided along with the NEXUS letter, but I do not share that opinion. First of all, the VA routinely uses Physician Assistants for conducting Compensation and Pension examinations at many VA Medical Centers and Clinics, so obviously, they don't require any "specialized training" for their doctors other than the levels of training required to be a physician assistant. Furthermore, the Veteran's doctor is doing him a favor by writing the NEXUS letter, so why would I recommend the Veteran insult him by asking how he is qualified to render a medical opinion that only requires a 50/50 percent probability? It doesn't make sense. He spent nearly 10 grueling years of schooling and medical training to earn the prestigious title of Medical Doctor. That in and of itself should be enough to qualify him to render an opinion. Obviously, if the doctor's qualifications or credentials are ever questioned by a Rater of Judge, then you will need to provide them, but I've never faced that situation and find it highly unlikely that you will either.

However, if you are using a specialist, it is important to select one that makes sense with regard to discussing your disability. For example, you wouldn't seek the opinion of a podiatrist to write a NEXUS letter regarding a pulmonary condition. Moreover, as mentioned earlier for mental disabilities, the NEXUS letter MUST come from a licensed psychologist or psychiatrist, and an audiologist for opinions regarding bilateral hearing loss and tinnitus.

Finally, in my humble opinion, each disability you claim should have its own NEXUS letter unless the conditions are specifically related, such as in the next chapter's scenario for low back and resulting leg pain. Although your physician may treat you for all the disabilities you claim, when you submit your claim to the VA, each disability is considered individually. Further, while the VA examiner may assess several of your conditions during your compensation and pension examination, he will address each one separately, giving opinions for each condition as he writes his final report.

Additionally, I believe you create better synergy when you establish a strong NEXUS for each condition, rather than trying to address them all in one very lengthy report. While you want your NEXUS letter to be thorough, you also want it to be as concise as possible because the Rater is trying to maintain his production numbers and working through these claims as quickly as he can. As such, if all relevant information for a particular disability is easy to review, then there is less chance for important facts to get overlooked.

Date

Typically the date would be the day the letter is signed by the doctor. If the doctor or a member of his staff types the NEXUS, then it will likely be included on the doctor's letterhead. However, in the event that you provide the letter on plain stationary, the doctor can write the date in ink at the time he signs the letter. Remember, this is a medical record and medical records should be date.

Identify the Patient

This is where we "establish" the relationship between the patient and the doctor and the purpose of the letter. I typically encourage the Veteran to ask his primary care doctor first, because he is most familiar with the Veteran's condition and treatment. But in the event you have to find a new doctor to provide the NEXUS letter, don't worry that the doctor does not have a long history with you. Remember, the compensation and pension examination will be the first time you will be seen by the VA examiner as well.

Information Reviewed

Fortunately, the VA helps you with determining what information your doctor needs to review to be able to provide a "balance of evidence" between his and the VA examiner's opinions. The VA lists the evidence they considered in their Rating Decision (or Statement of Case if your claim was denied on appeal) and the VA Examiner typically notes what he considered in his Compensation and Pension examination report. It's similar to the "discovery" a prosecutor must provide the defense team; this is where your doctor levels the playing field in formulating his opinion. But there are a few things you need to consider as you prepare your doctor's "qualifications."

First, you need to determine whether the information listed as "considered" by the VA was actually considered. As you will see in the hypothetical scenario listed in the next chapter, just because the VA itemizes "evidence considered," it doesn't necessarily mean that the Rater or Examiner actually reviewed it. When you submit information to the VA in support of your claim, the Claims Assistant or Veteran Service Representative is the person who actually logs it into your claim file, because they are responsible for the initial claim development. As such, if you feel that a piece of evidence you submitted is paramount to your claim and it's not specifically addressed in the denial, you will want to address that concern within your NEXUS letter.

Other considerations for this section are whether any evidence you submitted in support of your original claim is missing. The VA receives thousands of documents every day, so there is the possibility that your supporting evidence got misplaced or lost. If you don't see the evidence listed in the Rating Decision, you must assume that it wasn't reviewed (and by extension not considered) when the Rater made his decision.

Next, you should determine what additional evidence you have or need to acquire in response to the denial. When you submit a claim, the VA will submit a record request to the National Personnel Records Center (aka National Archives in St Louis, MO) to obtain your Service Treatment Records (STRs), DD-214, and other relevant personnel records as applicable. Was all the information you expected to be in your records retrieved during that request? If not, you will need to figure out how to obtain the information. The Bonus Chapter at the end of this book will provide numerous suggestions on how to remedy this problem.

Finally, if you are unable to provide your doctor with evidence that would be essential for him to make an informed, balanced opinion, address that lack of information head on. If the only thing your doctor can verify is "the Veteran advised that he was in a field training accident and treated by a field medic..." that statement can possibly be woven into other concession(s) the VA has already made that validates your contentions. Moreover, if a piece of evidence is irrelevant, state that it is not necessary for the doctor to establish it as fact in order to formulate an independent, knowledgeable conclusion. For example, if the VA concedes that you were subjected to acoustic trauma as a result of your job and the Examiner states that all your audiology exams during your time in the military were within normal limits, the fact that YOUR doctor did not look at your STRs to establish those facts are now irrelevant. Regardless of how ridiculous it may seem to emphasize the obvious, I encourage you to do it anyway so that you minimize the possibility of the Rater denying your reconsideration because he didn't think through the irrelevance of your doctor's failure to review that information.

Opinion

This is where your doctor writes his magic words, "at least as likely as not caused by, the result of, or aggravated by…" Typically, the doctor would be opining that your disability would be caused by your "military service," but in some instances, such as a secondary condition or an unusual circumstance, the doctor should be more specific with his wording.

For example, a widow wanted to claim service connected death for her deceased husband who died of Alzheimer's disease; she felt the onset of his condition was caused by his time as a member of the Army's boxing team. We found medical evidence that supported her contention, specifically that brain damage in boxers caused by repeated blows to the head has been linked to Alzheimer's disease. In this particular case, her doctor opinioned that "it was at least as likely as not that the Veteran's Alzheimer's disease was caused by, the result of, or at a minimum aggravated beyond natural progression by his boxing career in the U.S. Army."

As you can see in this example, the NEXUS letter makes more sense than if the doctor simply stated "caused by his military service." He further strengthened the letter by explaining that the Veteran did not appear to have a genetic predisposition to Alzheimer's disease, for none of his immediate family had been diagnosed with this disease.

Medical Evidence

This part of the NEXUS letter is key to your success. Often times, the VA examiner will make a statement such as, "there is no medical research that would support the finding that..." or reference a piece of research that is skewed. For example, I've helped many veterans who have submitted claims for low back condition secondary to a service connected knee. The most common reason for the VA examiner's denial is a 2005 study that purports the assertion "there must be at least a 4-5 centimeter leg length discrepancy before an altered or antalgic gait can develop to the degree that would affect the hips or the back." If your doctor cannot find a piece of medical research that at least addresses why this isn't always accurate (it would be best if he could find evidence that would directly refute the Examiner's medical evidence!), the Rater will state that the VA examiner's opinion is more persuasive because he has medical research to support his opinion. Fortunately, the Internet is an amazing resource for finding relevant medical research!

To avoid the potential quagmire of who has the most credible medical research, I only search sources that have been "sanctioned" by the National Institute of Health or some other Governmental agency. If it comes from a .gov website, it would be difficult for the VA to argue that it wasn't a credible source of medical research. If possible, I try to find at least two different studies to establish my doctor's position as one of authority.

Moreover, when I cite medical research, I only use as much of the study as I need to support the doctor's argument. First of all, when it comes to NEXUS letters, you want it to be thorough, concise and as irrefutable as possible. If you've already proven your point, don't keep adding additional evidence that can possibly be contested. If even a small part of your doctor's argument can be refuted, it raises questions regarding the reliability of the rest of his supporting argument.

When I approach the task of finding supporting medical research, I google the topic and NIH to pull up results from the National Institute of Health. So for our example above, I would type something like "antalgic gait back pain NIH." You will see all kinds of links that discuss this topic. When I entered this search for the sake of providing an example for this book, the first nine suggestions had a .gov extension, indicating that it is a government website. Moreover, when you click on one of the links and begin reading the research, you will find links to other research related to that topic. Now, as you will see in the next chapter, as long as you cite your source, you can copy/paste the information directly into your NEXUS letter and then move onto your next section.

Acknowledge or Address Any Conflicting Opinions or Etiologies

I want to emphasize this point because I believe it is critical to establishing YOUR doctor as an equal, if not more credible source. In the example of the back denial we explored above, the conflict that needs to be addressed is the fact that the Examiner cites a study that reveals there must be a leg discrepancy of at least 4-5 centimeters before a gait becomes antalgic enough to affect the back. Obviously, this Veteran did not have a leg discrepancy that severe.

So in response to the Examiner's cited medical study, my Veteran's doctor argued that ANY antalgic gait, if left unchecked for an extended period of time will result in the same mechanical problems as with a leg length discrepancy. He then cited a study that revealed "the secondary gait changes observed among patients with osteoarthritis (OA) reflect a potential strategy to shift the body's weight more rapidly from the contralateral limb to the support limb" and "…increased loading rate in the lower extremity joints may lead to a faster progression of existing OA and to the onset of OA up the mechanical chain and into the lower back." As you can see in this example, the Veteran's doctor not only addressed the VA examiner's cited research as inconclusive for ALL secondary back problems, but then provided another study that explained why the Veteran's antalgic gate (caused by his service connected knee) resulted in his back disability.

Furthermore, it is also important to note any potential conflicting evidence up front so it doesn't come back to bite the Veteran during the Rater's reconsideration or review by the DRO or Appellate Judge. For example, in the case of the Army Boxer, when the Veteran separated from the Army, he gave up his boxing career, so the doctor mentioned that in the letter. But, if the Veteran would've continued his boxing career AFTER separating from the Army, then the doctor would've had to structure his opinion much differently.

To illustrate this point, a Navy Veteran developed asbestosis later in life and submitted a VA claim due to his exposure to asbestos while serving aboard WWII era ships. The VA denied his claim because the VA examiner opined that "it was less likely than not that the Veteran's asbestosis was caused by his 14 months aboard two different boats in the early 1950s, but more likely than not due to his exposure to asbestos during his 35+ year career as an auto mechanic after separating from the Navy." As such, the Examiner's opinion implied that the AMOUNT and CONCENTRATION LEVELS of asbestos exposure while on board a WWII boat, when compared to the those in an automotive shop were irrelevant considerations when he determined the probable etiology of this Veteran's disease.

When the Veteran's doctor wrote his NEXUS letter, he first had to address the significance in the amount and concentration levels between the Veteran's exposures during his military service and his career as a mechanic, and then explain how the "minimal" time the Veteran was exposed to significant levels of asbestos aboard the Navy vessels was far more damaging to his lungs than his "lengthy" career as a mechanic. In his closing statement, the doctor argued that the likelihood the Veteran inhaled extensive amounts of asbestos dust aboard ship (it was used as insolation on the pipes that ran directly above the Sailors' berthing!) was a more persuasive and likely etiology than the minimal amounts of asbestos dust he might've ingested from mechanical sources such as brake parts. By confronting the Examiner's argument and then presenting an equally compelling counter-argument, the Doctor's NEXUS provided an approximate balance of positive evidence AND invoked the "benefit of doubt" (reasonable doubt.)

Closing Statement – Reiterate Opinion

It may not be necessary, but I believe the closing paragraph makes it easier for the Rater to see the entire opinion encapsulated in just a few sentences, so that when he reads the Doctor's signature, he is left with the final impression that this letter approximates a balance of positive evidence. It reminds me of the old adage I learned when briefing my superiors: "Tell 'em what you're going to tell 'em; Tell 'em; then Tell 'em what you told 'em!"

Signature

Aside from stating a positive opinion, the signature is the most important element of your doctor's letter; without a qualifying medical provider's signature, this document is nothing more than a personal statement to the VA. Granted, in theory the Rater MAY ask the VA examiner to review your statement if you ask for reconsideration, but in reality there would be no compelling reason for the Rater to do so since he already obtained a medical opinion and your unsigned NEXUS letter would not carry the same weight (approximate a balance of positive evidence) as the VA examiner's opinion. At best, the only thing you could hope for on appeal is for an unsigned NEXUS letter to convince a DRO or a Judge to ask for another Medical opinion based upon the medical evidence or any missing evidence that wasn't considered. And if he does send the claim back to the Examiner, odds are not in your favor that you would get an unbiased opinion the second time around.

Doctor's Title and Medical Examiner Number

Including the Title and Medical Examiner Number after the doctor's signature is not necessarily a requirement, but it does lend an additional level of authority to the overall impression of the NEXUS letter. Each State has its own registry for certifying the doctors licensed and practicing within their State. If there is ever a question of the doctor's qualification, having the ME # listed will simply make it easy for the Rater to look him up in that State's registry. However, as in my earlier comment regarding a request for your doctor's specific qualifications to render a 50/50 percent opinion, if the doctor fails to list his title and/or number, I would submit the NEXUS anyway. If there is ever a reason to question the doctor's qualifications, the ME # can easily be retrieved.

So now that we've addressed the individual components, let's look at what all this would actually look like in a solid NEXUS letter.

Chapter 5

Putting it All Together

Now that we've looked at the anatomy of a NEXUS letter and broken down its individual components, let's consider what a solid NEXUS letter might look like using the following scenario as a reference:

SCENAREO: Mr. John Smith enlisted in the Army in January 2003 and served 5 years as an Airborne Ranger; he was discharged in January 2008. It is now 2018 and he struggles with daily activities due to his severe back and leg pain. He feels these disabilities were caused by the myriad number of jumps he performed while in the Army. He submitted a VA disability claim and provided private medical records, dated June 2015 to January 2018 that establishes a diagnosis of degenerative disc disease of the lumbar spine and bilateral radiculopathy of the lower extremities secondary to the lumbar spine.

Upon receipt of his claim, the VA requested his records from the National Personnel Records Center (aka National Archives in St Louis, MO) and scheduled him for a Compensation and Pension examination at a VA Medical Center near where he lived. Eventually, he received notification that the VA denied his claim. The Notification Letter was not very specific, so Mr. Smith went to the Release of Information Office at the VA Medical Center and requested a copy of his Compensation and Pension examination report.

After reviewing it, he learned that the VA examiner had confirmed his Doctor's diagnosis of degenerative disc disease of the lumbar spine with accompanying bilateral radiculopathy of his lower extremities.

The Examiner conceded that there was one entry in Mr. Smith's service treatment records from 2004 that documented "back strain," a 14 day prescription of ibuprofen, and a physical profile of limited duty for 30 days. He also noted that a comment of "injured back" was annotated on Mr. Smith's separation physical in 2008. Nonetheless, the Examiner specifically noted that there was no mention of radiculopathy or evidence of any further back treatment from 2004 until his separation in 2008 and that Mr. Smith had not provided any medical evidence of any additional back problems until 2015; over 7 years after his discharge and nearly 11 years since the documented back strain. As such, the VA examiner opined that because there was no documented chronicity of treatment from 2004 until 2015, the back strain noted in his service treatment records was likely resolved by the treatment prescribed.

Therefore, he concluded that Mr. Smith's claimed back disability was less likely than not caused by his military service. Moreover, since there was no mention of radiculopathy in his service treatment records, that condition could not be considered for service connection as a primary condition or as a secondary condition to the back, since the back was not connected to his military service.

Needless to say, Mr. Smith is disappointed with the VA's decision and wants to discuss this with his doctor to see if he will provide a NEXUS letter in support of his disability so he can resubmit his VA claim for reconsideration. His doctor agreed and wrote the following:

Dr. Elmer T. Fudd, MD

1234 Main Street

Back Holler, TN 38556

May 26, 2018

To Whom It May Concern:

Mr. Smith has been a patient of mine since June, 2015. I have been treating him for degenerative disc disease of the lumber spine and bilateral radiculopathy of the lower extremities due to disc compression on nerves in his lumbosacral joint (L5-S1). He has requested that I provide an opinion as to the etiology of his back and bilateral lower extremity problems, since he wishes to submit a disability claim to the VA. As such, I have reviewed Mr. Smith's prior service medical and military personnel records, VA Rating Decision dated 4/1/2018 and Compensation and Pension Examination dated 3/15/2018, private medical records from 6/2015 to present, relevant medical research, and his reported history.

Considering the sum of this evidence while following the etiology of his disabilities from their purported origin to date, I've concluded that it is at least as likely as not that Mr. Smith's current back condition was caused by, the result of, or aggravated by his military service. Moreover, I believe it is at least as likely as not that his bilateral lower extremity radiculopathy is caused by, the result of, or aggravated by his back condition.

Mr. Smith reports that while in the Military, he was a young, strong paratrooper with a "gung-ho" attitude who rarely complained of physical ailments; his DD-214 verifies that he was awarded a Parachutist Badge. However, he stated that after one particularly difficult jump in 2004, he visited the clinic due to injuring his back and was prescribed pain medication and light duty for a period of 30 days. This statement was verified by the VA Examiner in his examination report dated 3/15/2018.

Mr. Smith reported that he was ridiculed by his peers during this convalescence period and decided he would never willingly return to the clinic for back pain out of pride and the possibility of being removed from ready jump status.

Moreover, Mr. Smith reports that after that injury in 2004, his back bothered him sporadically, especially after intense physical activity and continued to worsen as he aged. However, he stated that he could not afford medical insurance for several years after separating from the military, so he routinely self-medicated with extra-strength Tylenol and other over-the-counter medication, ice, heat, and rest when his back pain flared. This explanation ostensibly explains the lack of medical evidence in support of a chronic disability claim for several years during and post military service.

X-rays of Mr. Smith's back in 2015 revealed significant degenerative disc disease, consistent with a 14+ year old injury. Although these private medical records are listed under "Evidence Considered" in the VA Rating Decision dated 4/1/2018, it is unclear whether the VA examiner actually considered them, for there is no mention of their relevance (or lack thereof) in his report. It appears that once he determined that "the back strain noted in his service treatment records was likely resolved by the treatment prescribed," he neglected to consider any other possibilities as to the etiology of Mr. Smith's disability.

Nevertheless, in a recent National Institute of Health's (NIH) study located in the Public Medical Database titled, "Evaluation and Management of Vertebral Compression Fractures," it is noted that "vertebral compression injuries have an insidious onset and may produce only low-grade back pain initially. Over time, the injury often leads to progressive loss of stature and continuous contraction of the paraspinal musculature to maintain posture. This combination results in fatigued muscles and pain that often continues even after the original compression injury has healed. This research is consistent with the 2004 entry in Mr. Smith's medical records that indicates "back strain."

In another study located in the NIH medical library titled, "Cervical spine injury patterns in three modes of high-speed trauma: a biomechanical porcine model," 16 three-vertebrae segments were subjected to flexion-compression, extension-compression, and compression-alone trauma modes, with the results analyzed for variance with trauma mode using nonparametric analysis. The three modes of trauma were found to have statistically significant degrees of injury to the spine and its structural components, with the severity of anatomic injuries in these models relating most to the addition of bending moments to high-speed axial compression of the spine segment, such as that demonstrated by the movements associated with paratrooper jump activities.

Given the research mentioned above, coupled with Mr. Smith's medical history, rigors of military service in the field and during training, such as jumping out of airplanes and forced marches, the nature of compression type injury and it's resulting degenerative disc disease, chronicity of arthralgia and lack of any other obvious etiology, I believe it is at least as likely as not that his back condition was caused by, the result of or aggravated by his military service and the resulting radiculopathy a byproduct of the injured back.

If you have any questions regarding this opinion, you can email me at ETFudd@fuddspineinstitute.com or call my assistant, Jenny at 867-5309.

Respectfully,

Elmer T. Fudd

Elmer T. Fudd, MD, ME#2534263

As you can see, this sample NEXUS letter addresses all the components listed in Chapter 4 and would make it hard for any Rater, DRO, or Judge to argue that equipoise has not been established. Moreover, according to CFR 38, he would have to grant this claim based upon the Benefit of Doubt doctrine. But does this example truly reflect reality? For some of you, reading this sample NEXUS letter may be all that you needed to resurrect your claim or appeal, for now that you know what is needed in to create reasonable doubt, you can discuss your claim with your doctor and he will write (or you can write and present for him to sign) a winning NEXUS letter.

But for the rest of you, this knowledge may only add to your frustration; how will I ever be able to find a doctor who will write or even sign a NEXUS letter like that?

As we discussed in Chapter 3, a big concern that many doctors have is that they don't want to write an opinion that will hurt your chances of winning your claim and their time is how they make their money. Moreover, drafting a NEXUS letter of the quality needed to invoke equipoise takes considerable time; he would have to dissect how and why the Rater and Examiner denied your claim, determine whether additional evidence needs to be acquired, and conduct medical research to support an opinion that would provide an approximate balance of positive evidence to the VA examiner's opinion. That is asking a lot of a Doctor! There are a few doctors out there who advertise that they will write you a solid NEXUS letter, but they charge as much as $5,000 and won't guarantee your success in winning your claim!

So what do you do if your doctor tells you he will sign whatever you provided him, as long as the he agrees with what you wrote? I've found that the key to getting a doctor to feel comfortable signing your NEXUS letter is to craft it in such a way that he would not be embarrassed to sign it (it must sound like it was written by a medical professional.) Secondly, the medical research you select to support his opinion must be relevant and not taken out of context. And lastly, allow him to feel as if he's helping you obtain an entitlement that you've earned and not helping you to "beat the system" for free benefits you don't deserve.

When I was a VSO and wrote NEXUS letters for my Veterans to present to their doctor, I would also write a brief explanation on how signing the letter would not negatively impact him or his practice and that we only needed a 50/50 percent probability of medical certainty. Then I always included the following in my closing statement; "This opinion/rationale is paramount for Mr. Smith to be eligible for VA compensation benefits, which I believe he has earned due to the selfless service he provided our country. Thank you in advance for your consideration." If Mr. Smith was humming a patriotic toon while the doctor was reading it, all the better!

If, after you present your NEXUS letter to your doctor he is still hesitant to accept your letter, or he modifies it beyond the standard needed to create equipoise, you may need to cut your losses, move on to another doctor and try again (Chapter 3 discusses ways to do this.)

Over the years, I've seen numerous NEXUS letters; all made good examples, unfortunately most of them were examples of how NOT to write a NEXUS letter. I've studied the good ones to determine what made them good, and the bad ones to determine why they were lacking. The sample letter above is the culmination of what I've learned. Feel free to modify that letter as needed for your own purposes, for if you are able to provide all the components we discussed, you will be able approximate a balance of positive evidence, invoke the benefit of doubt doctrine, and win your claim.

I would be very interested in hearing of your success. If there is something that I've written that is not clear, I would like to know that too. Please reach out to me via email and I will respond as soon as possible. rickblairbooks@gmail.com.

Now that I am retired, I do consult with Veterans who want personalized guidance with their Nexus letter(s.)   If you are having difficulty crafting your NEXUS letter, reach out to me at rickblairbooks@gmail.com and we can discuss your specific need.

* * *

PERSONAL REQUEST

I humbly ask that if you feel that this book has been beneficial to you in learning how to write a winning NEXUS letter, that you write a **POSITIVE REVIEW** so that others might be convinced that they too, can obtain the VA benefits they deserve.

Bonus Chapter

Locating Missing Records and Obtaining Supporting Evidence

If you find that you need to locate missing records or obtain additional supporting evidence, it may seem like a daunting task. How are you going to prove an injury that was treated by a field medic during a training exercise that was never documented? In a situation like this, you will have no choice but to get CREATIVE.

Do you remember the name of the medic or other buddies in your unit who can write a statement for you describing your injury and how it happened? Did you take a picture of something that could help corroborate your story? Did you write a letter home that could be used to establish a fact?

Although the VA has a duty to assist you in developing your claim, that duty only goes so far. The following ideas of how to get creative in your search for evidence to support your claim comes from my personal experience and those of my peers. I hope they inspire your imagination so that you can find the supporting evidence you need to win your claim. If you have any other ideas to add to this list, please share them with me so I can pass them along in subsequent books.

The VA Duty to Assist

Although it's ultimately up to you to prove your claim, according to the Code of Federal Regulations Title 38 (CFR), the VA has a duty to assist you in gathering the information you need. So what does that really mean? The VA has:

• A Duty to Notify the Veteran of Information Necessary to Complete their Application

• A Duty to Notify the Veteran of the Information and Evidence necessary to substantiate their claim.

- A Duty to Assist the Veteran in obtaining information

Duty to Notify Veteran of Information Necessary to Complete His Application

The VA has a duty to notify you of necessary information or evidence, except when a claim cannot be substantiated because there is no legal basis for the claim, or undisputed facts render the claimant ineligible for the claimed benefit. This includes which information and evidence, if any, you are to provide to VA and which information and evidence, if any, VA will try to obtain for you.

The information the VA says you need to provide must be submitted within one year of the date of the claim or the VA will adjudicate your claim based upon the information it has in your claim file. NOTE: the VA gives you 30 days to provide the information you need to provide. After that 30 days, they may go ahead and rate your claim, but if you provide the information within the one year period, the VA must award your claim back to the original date of claim.

If VA receives an incomplete application for benefits, it will notify you of the information necessary to complete the application and will defer assistance until you submit this information. If the information necessary to complete the application is not received by VA within one year from the date of such notice, your claim dies and you will have to start all over.

After the VA receives a complete or a substantially complete application for benefits, the VA is required to assist in the development of the claim. The Veterans Claims Assistance Act of 2000 (VCAA) requires the VA to notify the claimant of any information or medical or lay evidence that is needed to substantiate the claim. The VA is also obligated to inform the claimant about which information the VA will try to obtain on the claimant's behalf and which information or evidence the claimant will be required to obtain for himself.

Duty to assist the Veteran in Obtaining Information

The VA will make reasonable efforts to assist you in obtaining evidence necessary to substantiate your claim. Yes, that is a broad statement. The CFR states that the VA is not required to provide assistance to you if no reasonable possibility exists that such assistance would aid in substantiating the claim. However, the VA is required to assist you with obtaining private medical records. While this takes a long time within the VA, if your provider is going to charge you per page for your records, often times, they will provide them free of charge to the VA.

The VA is also responsible for obtaining your service medical records and, if you have records that are held or maintained by a governmental entity, they will try to help you get those records. Finally, the VA is responsible for providing a medical exam or obtaining a medical opinion when they feel an examination or opinion is necessary to make a decision on the claim.

National Archives

The National Personnel Records Center (NPRC) in St Louis, MO archives historical military personnel records and medical records of nearly 100 million veterans; the vast majority of these records are paper-based and not available on-line. Remarkably, the NPRC is quite proficient at processing the 1.4 million annual requests they receive each year and their archival practices and processes are amazing.

There are two ways to request your military records, first you can submit an SF-180 Request Pertaining To Military Records form (Google has links to this downloadable form) and mail it to National Personnel Records Center, Military Personnel Records, 1 Archives Drive, St. Louis, MO 63138 (NPRC Phone Number:314-801-0800, NPRC Fax Number: 314-801-9195.) Second, you can submit your request online at https://www.archives.gov/veterans/military-service-records. According to the NPRC website, when requesting records, it is extremely helpful to NPRC staff if you provide the purpose or reason for your request, such as applying for veterans benefits or researching your personal military history.

NOTE: in 1973, there was a fire at the National Personnel Records Center that damaged or destroyed an estimated 16-18 million Army and Air Force records that documented the service history of former military personnel discharged from 1912-1964. Although the information in many of these primary source records was either badly damaged or completely destroyed, the NPRC's official line is that "often alternate record sources can be used to reconstruct the service of the veterans impacted by the fire. Sometimes we are able to reconstruct the service promptly using alternate records that are in our holdings, but other times we must request information from other external agencies for use in records reconstruction. In some instances, therefore, requests that involve reconstruction efforts may take several weeks to a month to complete."

My experience in working with Veterans who were affected by lost or missing records is that the process of trying to "recreate" those records is rarely this simple or positive. In the event your records cannot be located, they will send you a form asking for any information that would help them recreate your records, such as time periods, units you served in, etc., which most of us don't remember. If you are one of the Veterans whose records were lost in this fire or misplaced and can't be found, then you will need to hope that you can find alternative sources to provide the evidence needed to support your claim.

Here are a few online resources that are mentioned on the NPRC website that may also be helpful to you in recreating your records:

Online Veterans and Military Documents

https://www.archives.gov/research/military/veterans/online - This is a link of digital archives for Current Era Operations, Vietnam War, Korean War, WWII, WWI, Spanish-American War, Civil War, and Revolutionary War.

Genealogy and Military Records.

https://www.archives.gov/research/military/genealogy.html - This site is more helpful to genealogy research, but it does have links to military sites that may be helpful, if only to lead you to another site that is helpful (six degrees of Kevin Bacon?)

National Archives Catalog.

https://www.archives.gov/research/military/veterans/arc.html - This link is primarily a digitized listing of images of documents and photos. There majority of the links are of WWII war casualties, but there may be some gems in there if your records were destroyed in the fire.

Buddy Statements

This is what the VA calls any personal letter in support of a Veteran's claim, regardless of who wrote it (spouse, child, peer, Commanding Officer, etc.) Typically, this evidence is not given much weight by Raters and DROs, but often carries much more weight with an Appellate Judge. The more specific your Buddy can be in his letter, the better chance you will have in your attempt to approximate a positive balance of evidence; in some cases it could mean tipping the scales in the Veteran's favor.

Military Awards/Decoration Citation and Performance Reviews

The write ups in these documents can sometimes contain hidden gems in trying to establish a fact in support of your claim. Some of you may recall that there was a time during the Vietnam War that admin folks were instructed not to state RVN or Vietnam on documents, but to call it Southeast Asia or SEA. As such, it made it impossible to actually prove Vietnam service, because there were other areas within "SEA" that were not sprayed with Agent Orange. This was the case with one of my Veterans who was stationed in Japan, we could not find any documentation that he'd been sent TDY to Vietnam. However, his supervisor had included a bullet in his performance reports stating the Veteran provided crucial "hands on support" to a sister unit during a certain timeframe that helped them succeed their mission. We were able to establish the fact that the sister unit had been deployed to Vietnam during that specific time frame, so by extension, the Veteran had to have had "boots on ground" and VA granted his presumptive disability.

NOTE: Although you may have been awarded a Vietnam Service Medal, Vietnam Campaign Medal, Armed Forces Expeditionary Medal and/or the Vietnam Cross of Gallantry, these awards are not acceptable proof of Vietnam service for the purpose of proving herbicide exposure. The Vietnam Service Medal was awarded to service members who were stationed on ships offshore or flew high altitude missions over the Vietnam as well as those who served in Thailand. The Armed Forces Expeditionary Medal was issued by all branches of the service during the years before 1965 and may indicate duty or visitation in Vietnam, however it must be corroborated by documentation of travel or TDY orders to Vietnam. The Vietnam Cross of Gallantry was issued by the Vietnamese Government to all units subordinate to Military Assistance Command (MACV) and the U.S. Army Vietnam, regardless of their physical presence in Vietnam. Since this is a unit-level citation and not an individual citation, receipt of this medal alone is not acceptable proof of service in Vietnam.

Physical Profiles

This is a source of information that is often overlooked.

Occasionally a physical profile can be found in medical records, but typically they are located in the personnel file, because it affects the Veteran's ability to be fit for worldwide deployment. Moreover, it is specifically referenced when it comes time for a Veteran to meet his physical fitness standards. As such, the profile must be specific in determining which matrixes are waived (i.e., no running or walking, but pushups and sit-ups are authorized) and often lists the reason for the waiver (i.e., sprained knee.) If you've ever needed a profile, you know that the injured troop must go to sick call so the doctor can evaluate whether he needs a waiver for physical training. It's not uncommon for the doctor to quickly fill out a profile form for the Veteran to submit the First Sergeant without documenting it in the Veteran's medical record.

Naval Cruise books

Granted, this is not a common source for useful supporting evidence, but I recall a situation where a Navy Veteran was aboard a Vessel and became ill while at a port of call in Japan. His ship left port while he was still hospitalized, so when he finished his convalescence, the Navy had to figure out what to do with him. He was offered the opportunity to go back to the States or join another Vessel that was on its way to Vietnam that had stopped in Japan for supplies. The Veteran elected to join this Vessel and remain at sea for the duration of his enlistment.

During the course of that cruise, the Vessel traversed the intercostal waterways of Vietnam, which qualified him for presumptive disabilities due to Agent Orange exposure. However, his transfer to that Vessel was never documented in his personnel records and he separated from the Navy upon its return to the U.S. Fortunately for this Veteran, he was aboard this Vessel while pictures were taken to create a cruise book. He obtained a copy of the cruise book (it's amazing what you can find on eBay!) and the VA granted his claim based upon the photographic evidence in that book.

Unit Histories and Log Books

This is a fairly lucrative source of information to establish facts if you can find them. Fortunately, more and more of these historical documents are being located in the archives and posted online. I recall a Veteran who was on his way from the U.S. to the Philippines and his aircraft had to make an emergency stop at Da Nang Air Base. He was there for three or four days while the aircraft was repaired. When he arrived and signed into his duty station in the Philippines, it was noted in the unit log. Fortunately for this Veteran, when he obtained a copy of that unit log book (I don't recall how or where he found a copy), a log entry a few days prior to his reporting for duty noted that he'd not signed into the unit as scheduled, because there had been a mechanical delay at Da Nang Air Base while in route to his duty station.

Photos

Typically, if a Veteran can provide photographic evidence that CLEARLY establishes a fact, the VA will accept that evidence in support of their claim. I emphasize CLEARLY, because if there is no way to connect the Veteran to the fact that he's trying to prove, it is merely an interesting photo. I recall a number of Veterans who were trying to prove they were in Vietnam by providing pictures of themselves with buddies standing in from of thatch huts or some similar type of photos that depicted nothing identifiable to prove that picture was taken in Vietnam as opposed to any other SEA country. However, I did have a Veteran who was a member of a Radar repair crew that would travel from site to site along the DMZ to service the radars. His claim was initially denied because his unit of assignment was several miles from the DMZ, so the VA stated that he had not been exposed to Agent Orange.

The Veteran provided a picture of himself and two other GIs standing next to a radar at an outpost that was located on the DMZ. At first glance, the picture seemed to be nothing more than a couple of GI buddies standing next to some unknown equipment in a barren, unidentified landscape. Initially, the VA stated that the picture was inconclusive proof that he was ever on the DMZ. Through intense Internet research (how did we ever function before the Internet?), we found unit histories (including photos) that cited the specific radar equipment and their locations along the Korean DMZ. Comparing that verifiable information with his picture, we were able to establish that he was standing next to a specific radar at a specific location on the DMZ that established that he had indeed been subjected to Agent Orange exposure.

Newspaper Articles

In decades past, it used to be common practice for small town newspapers to write a story on their "Home Town Heroes." One of my Veterans had been in the Army Reserves back in the 1970s and was injured in a car accident on the way home from a weekend drill. According to the CFR, a Reservist is considered "on Active Duty" from the time he leaves his home until he returns home during a weekend drill period. He was injured pretty badly and treated at the local hospital, but those private medical records were long destroyed. His military personnel records revealed multiple missed drill weekends after his purported accident and subsequent dismissal from the Reserves for failure to participate, but no explanation accompanied these records. Fortunately, he was able to provide a newspaper clipping that quoted a police report regarding the accident that established the date and time of the accident (it even had a picture of his mangled car wrapped around a tree!) We were then able to cross-reference that information with his Reserve Participation Log to establish that he'd been on duty at his unit on that day, so the VA granted his claim.

Letters to Family

Letters to family have helped numerous Veterans in establishing that an event happened in service. I recall a Veteran who submitted a presumptive claim for an Agent Orange related disability, but couldn't find any evidence to show that he'd been TDY to Vietnam.

He was a helicopter mechanic from the Guam who had been appointed at the last minute to be a part of a team to fix a number of choppers at Tan Son Nhut Air Base. As such, he was included on blanket TDY orders for the unit that didn't specifically list his name and he wasn't added to any flight manifests since he literally grabbed his go bag and jumped on the plane. Fortunately for him, his wife of 40+ years had been his girlfriend when he was in the military and she'd kept a letter that he'd sent from Tan Son Nhut Air Base. The post mark on that envelop was sufficient evidence to establish "boots on ground" in Vietnam and his claim was granted.

Social media

Last but not least, social media is an amazing tool for reuniting us with people that we've lost touch with decades in the past. I came from a small town in Indiana with a graduating class of less than 200. Facebook has allowed me to reestablish friendships that had become a far distant memories due to passing time and countless miles. This has become an especially powerful medium to network with others from the past who can help you establish facts and find evidence. I could not tell you how many Veterans have used social media to not only obtain the evidence they needed to win their claims, but reestablished connections that have helped them come to terms with some of the difficulties they experienced while in service. The healing that I've witnessed in these Veterans that have resulted from these reconnections have been truly inspiring.

I would be very interested in hearing of your success. If there is something that I've written that is not clear, I would like to know that too. Please reach out to me via email and I will respond as soon as possible. rickblairbooks@gmail.com.

* * *

Now that I am retired, I do consult with Veterans who want personalized guidance with their Nexus letter(s.) If you are having difficulty crafting your NEXUS letter, reach out to me at rickblairbooks@gmail.com and we can talk about your specific need.

* * *

$*\quad*\quad*$

PERSONAL REQUEST

I humbly ask that if you feel that this book has been beneficial to you in learning how to write a winning NEXUS letter, that you write a **POSITIVE REVIEW** so that others might be convinced that they too, can obtain the VA benefits they deserve.

☐

$*\quad*\quad*$

Made in the USA
Columbia, SC
06 January 2020